ROCK THAT QUILT BLOCK :HOURGLASS

LINDA J. HAHN

The American Quilter's Society or AQS is dedicated to quilting excellence. AQS promotes the triumphs of today's quilter, while remaining dedicated to the quilting tradition. We believe in the promotion of this art and craft through AQS Publishing and AQS QuiltWeek®.

CONTENT EDITOR: CAITLIN TETREV
TECHNICAL EDITOR: EMMY WALTON
GRAPHIC DESIGN: CHRIS GILBERT AND ELAINE WILSON
COVER DESIGN: MICHAEL BUCKINGHAM
HOW-TO PHOTOGRAPHY: LINDA J. HAHN
QUILT PHOTOGRAPHY: CHARLES R. LYNCH
ASSISTANT EDITOR: ADRIANA FITCH
DIRECTOR OF PUBLICATIONS: KIMBERLY HOLLAND TETREV

Additional copies of this book may be ordered from the American Quilter's Society, PO Box 3290, Paducah, KY 42002-3290, or online at www.ShopAQS.com.

American Quilter's Society
www.AmericanQuilter.com

Library of Congress Cataloging-in-Publication Data

PENDING

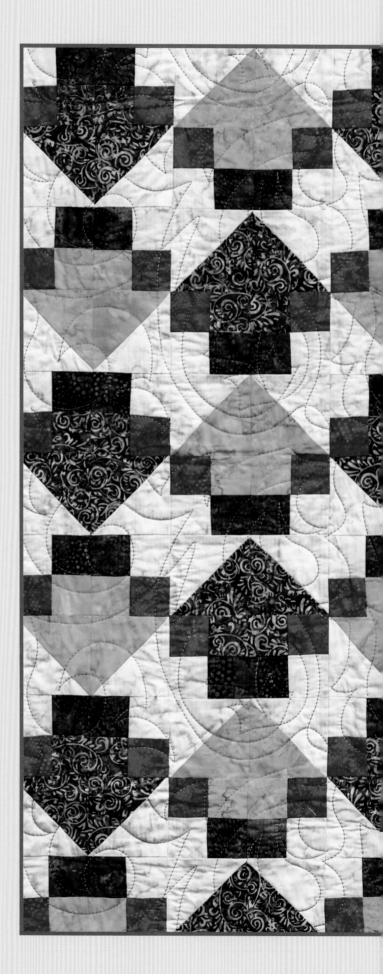

DEDICATION

work a lot, maybe more than I should. At least five days a week, I "turn off the world" for an hour and head off to Zumba. Where I not only dance, but laugh….a lot. I dance with a group of ladies who have become very dear and cherished friends. Whoever said laughter is the best medicine is spot on!

This book is dedicated to girls from the Freehold Zumba Crew – Debbie Mack and Marla Rae Thorn, my teachers, my mentors, and most importantly my friends. To the rest of the crew – Susan Yonus, Eva Colosi, Kerri McCabe, Jackie Barendregt, Carol Lippen, Sarah Hazel, Mary Holtz, Trisha Dungo, Tracey Lashley, Dee Dee Amedu, and "TJ" Brandon. I dedicate this to you.

I love my Zumba family!

COVER QUILT: FIVE O'CLOCK SOMEWHERE, detail, full quilt on p. 56.

TITLE PAGE: TIME TRAVEL , detail, full quilt on p. 46.

LEFT: RAIN DELAY , detail, full quilt on p. 67.

ACKNOWLEDGMENTS

Thank you to my awesome piecing team—Deborah Stanley, Rebecca Szabo, Nancy Rock, Anna Marie Ameen, Janet Byard, Debbie Welch, Debbie Fetch, Melissa Winters, and LuAnne Halleran.

Heartfelt thanks to longarm quilters – Jodi Robinson and Deloa Jones. Your beautiful quilting makes the quilts even more stunning!

Thank you to Deb and Jim Welch of Quilting Possibilities™, Judy and Rob Engime of Olde City Quilts™ for your continued support and most importantly, your friendship.

Special thanks to the companies who generously shared their products with me for the book—Steady Betty, Triangles on a Roll, Hoffman California, Timeless Treasures, Island Batik, Fairfield Processing, Cheryl Ann's Design Wall, Panasonic, and Aurifil. Huge thanks to BERNINA for the awesome BERNINA 580!

I thank my very dear friends, Linda M. Poole, Mickey Depre, and Suzan Ellis for your continued support and friendship.

Thank you to Kimberly Tetrev, Publishing Director and Caitlin Tetrev and the entire amazing staff at the American Quilter's Society for once again bringing my newest concept to life! You all ROCK!

Thank you to my family, my husband Allan, my daughter Sarah, and my sister Susan Stillinger for your love and support through this process. I could not do it without you.

CONTENTS

INTRODUCTION

Welcome to Book #2 in the ROCK THAT QUILT BLOCK series! In this book, we will be rocking the Hourglass block!

One of the things I really enjoy is taking a specific block and playing with it. I play with color placement, rotating the blocks, or rotating the patches within the block.

In presenting this series, I hope to encourage you to step outside of your box, to play and try different construction methods and layouts for a specific block.

I would like to think that this is not just a pattern book, but also a TEACHING book.

As you go through this book, please take note of the names of the quilts. All the quilt names have a common theme...Time.

So let's go **ROCK THAT QUILT BLOCK!**

Linda

 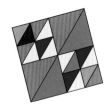

GENERAL HINTS

Stitch length

Always remember that you *may* have to rip something out so you do not want a stitch length that is so tight that you will rip the fabric!

Fabric Yardage

The yardage stated for each of the quilts is GENEROUS. This takes into consideration fabric shrinkage, cuts that end up being short and of course, mis-cuts! Nobody is perfect, it happens to me, too! I would much rather purchase a little extra fabric now, than have to try to locate a fabric, after the fact.

The backing fabric yardage assumes that you will be piecing the backing together with a vertical seam. Also included in that calculation is enough backing for a matching hanging sleeve, which is also enough in the event that you send your quilt to a long arm quilter.

Starching and Pressing

To starch or not to starch is a matter of personal preference. That said, I am a starcher! I think that starching gives the seams a good crisp finish.

I starch before I cut and while I am piecing, I starch the pieces that I have stitched and then let the starch dry before pressing.

STARCHED IS GOOD – CRISPY IS BETTER

Chain Piecing

I chain piece whenever possible. Make one block to get the technique down, chain piece as much as you can.

The Piecing Factor

Everyone has their own personal thoughts when it comes to piecing. Some folks choose to rip if the seams are one thread off of perfection, others may choose not to. I respect both choices and all in between. I am not perfect, my quilts are not perfect.

Terminology and Abbreviations

Throughout this book, I will use some terminology and abbreviations—so please read through them before you start on a project.

* RST: Right sides of the fabrics together
* RSU: Right side of the fabric up
* RSD: Right side of the fabric down
* HST: Half Square Triangles
* TOAR: Triangles on a Roll
* WOF: Width of Fabric (across the fabric approximately 42" +/-)
* Finished: the size of the patch after it is stitched on all four sides
* Unfinished: the size that you cut the patch (finished size + ¼" seam allowance on all four sides)

MATERIALS AND SUPPLIES
Stuff I Can't Live Without

While I am all about simplicity and minimal tools, there are some things I just can't live without. They make my quilt making activities stress free.

Triangles on a Roll

There are many different half square triangle products on the market, but this is by far my favorite. When working with this product, I usually try to work with as much as I can easily handle at a time.

Purchase the FINISHED size of triangles that you wish to make.

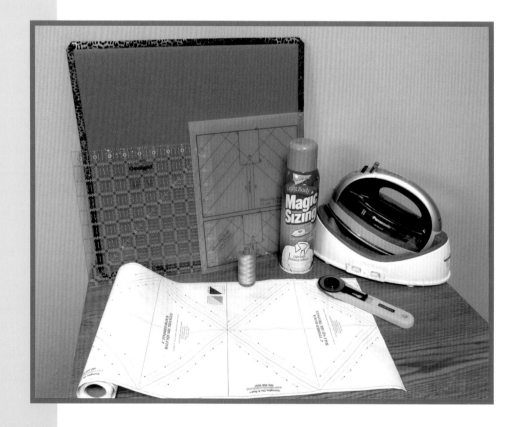

Starch—Magic Sizing

I'm a huge fan of starch. It is my opinion that my seams are much crisper and the fabric doesn't stretch as much during the pressing process.

Steady Betty Board

I use the 16" board size. It's great to design on as the pieces won't move. You can also press on the board and not distort your pieces.

Omnigrid 9½" square

Absolute favorite ruler EVER! I can pretty much do everything with a 9½" square and a 6" x 24" ruler. This square fits my hand without slipping and can fit in my purse.

Aurifil 50 wt. Cotton

I always piece with a quality cotton thread, such as Aurifil. I use either cream or taupe.

Panasonic Cordless Iron

Love that there is NO cord (fig. 1)!

Cheryl Ann Design Wall

I keep this cute 18" square portable design wall (fig. 2), up on my sewing desk, so I can pin the components to it as I get them pieced together.

What's My Angle

"The WMA tool (fig. 3) allows you to make connector squares really quickly and accurately. You can even chain piece with this tool!"

You get two tools in one package—one for your home machine and one for your take to class machine!

Fig. 1

Fig. 2

Fig. 3

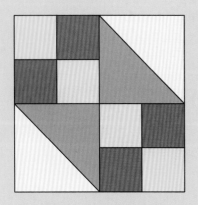

Fig. 1

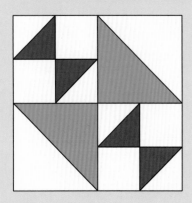

Fig. 2

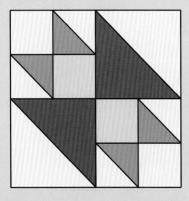

Fig. 3

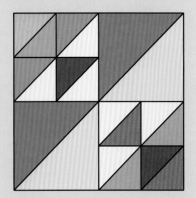

Fig. 4

BREAKING DOWN THE BLOCK

The Basic Hourglass block consists of two (2) Four Patch and two (2) Half Square Triangle, (fig. 1).

It can easily be made into 4", 6", 8", 9", and 12" finished squares. Other sizes would require cutting in ⅛" increments. Since most quilters are not particularly fond of doing that, I will stick with the block sizes that are quilter friendly (fig. 2).

Block Size	Four Patch Cutting	Half Square Triangle Cutting
4"	Cut 1½" squares	Cut 3" squares
6"	Cut 2" squares	Cut 4" squares
8"	Cut 2½" squares	Cut 5" squares
9"	Cut 2¾" squares	Cut 5½" squares
12"	Cut 3" squares	Cut 4" squares

Here is a variation on the Hourglass. Instead of a plain Four Patch—we will substitute two (2) Half Square Triangles (fig. 3).

Let's change the position of the small HST units and change the color of one (1) of the solid squares to make another variation. (fig. 4).

Now let's make the Four Patch all small HST units and rotate the larger HST a quarter turn.

CALCULATIONS
For Using Triangles on a Roll (TOAR)

Calculations for using 4" finished TOAR
Pair with 2" Finished TOAR

Strip width = 10½"

Number of Squares	Yields number of HST	Size to cut for TOAR
2 (1 x 2)	4	10½" x 5½"
4 (2 x 2)	8	10½" x 10½"
6 (2 x 3)	12	10½" x 15½"
8 (4 x 4)	16	10½" x ½ WOF
16 (2 x 8)	32	10½" x WOF

Calculations for using 3" finished TOAR
Pair with 1½" Finished TOAR

Strip width = 8½"

Number of Squares	Yields number of HST	Size to cut for TOAR
4 (2 x 2)	8	8½" x 8½"
6 (2 x 3)	12	8½" x 12"
8 (2 x 4)	16	8½" x 16½"
10 (2 x 5)	20	8½" x ½ WOF
20 (2 x WOF)	40	8½" x WOF

Calculations for using 2" finished TOAR
Pair with 4" Finished TOAR

Strip width = 6½"

Number of Squares	Yields number of HST	Size to cut for TOAR
2 (2 x 2)	4	6½" x 6½"
6 (2 x 3)	12	6½" x 9½"
8 (2 x 4)	16	6½" x 12"
12 (2 x 6)	24	6½" x 24"
14 (2 x 7)	28	6½" x ½ WOF
20 (2 x 13)	52	8½" x WOF

Calculations for using 1½" finished TOAR
Pair with 3" Finished TOAR

Strip width = 10½"

Number of Squares	Yields number of HST	Size to cut for TOAR
4 (4 x 1)	8	10½" x 3"
8 (4 x 2)	16	10½" x 5½"
12 (4 x 3)	24	10½" x 8"
16 (4 x 4)	32	10½" x 10½"
36 (4 x 9)	72	10½" x ½ WOF
68 (4 x 17)	136	10½" x WOF

Fig. 1. Draw diagonal line from corner to corner—stitch scant ¼" on each side. Chain piece in alternating directions

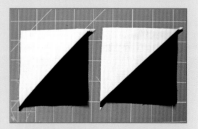

Fig. 2. Cut apart on drawn line and press to the dark.

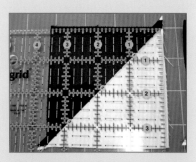

Fig. 3. Place the ruler on the triangle putting the diagonal line on the seam allowance and sliver trim.

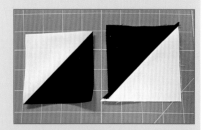

Fig. 4. Trim evenly distributes fabric on both sides.

TECHNIQUES

Half Square Triangles (HST)

There are several different ways to make half square triangles (referred to as HST in this book).

We are most familiar with the method of drawing a diagonal line from corner to corner and stitching a scant ¼" away from the line (fig. 1)—cutting apart on the line and trimming to the desired size (fig. 2)—so let's start there!

When using this method, I do not use measurements with ⅞"—rather, I round up ⅛" and work with whole numbers. For example, if I want my HST to be 2" finished—I will cut my squares 3"–1" larger than the desired finished size

Trim to the desired UNFINISHED size by placing the diagonal line on the ruler in the seam allowance (fig. 3) (which equally distributes the fabric on both sides, figure 4).

Using Triangles on a Roll

By far, my favorite way of making (HST) is by using a product called Triangles on a Roll. You must purchase them by the finished size that you wish your (HST) to be. I do use them slightly different than the directions on the package.

Fig. 5

When you are getting used to working with triangle paper, it may help you to number the (HST's) that you will need (fig. 5).

I prefer working with a (WOF) cut in half if at all possible. It is just easier to manipulate under the sewing machine.

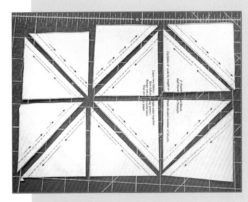

Fig. 6

I prefer to extend the fabric slightly beyond the paper so I have something to hold on to when stitching—thus I add a ½" on to the recommended (WOF) on the (TOAR) paper (fig. 6).

Place the fabric that you are pressing toward (RSU) on the bottom and the fabric you are pressing away from (RSD). Spritz with starch and press the two fabrics together.

Roll out the paper and pin securely.

Stitch following the arrows on the paper, remove the pins as you go.

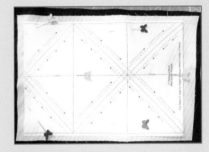

Fig. 7

When you have completed stitching, I like to press the wrong side to set the stitches.

Take the triangle fabric to the cutting board and cut apart on the drawn lines (fig. 7). Here's a great time to practice Power Cutting!

Take the triangles that you just stitched over to the ironing board and place them paper side down. One by one, take each triangle and press closed—and then press open—WITH the paper ON. Leaving the paper on provides a little more stability (fig. 8).

Fig. 8

Now it's time to clip the bunny ears and then remove the paper.

Your perfect triangles are now good to go!

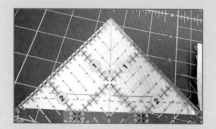

Fig. 9

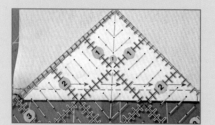

Fig. 10

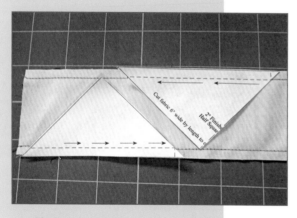

Fig. 11

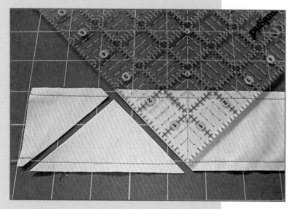

Fig. 12

No Squares?? No Problem

Draw out the size triangle that you need on a piece of paper and cut it apart. (You can also just cut a section off from the TOAR for this step as well).

Measure from the edge to the point. Add ¼" to that measurement if you'd like (fig. 9).

Stitch two strips (yes, strips) that have been cut the width of your measurement plus the ¼" (fig. 10).

Place the triangle on the strip - matching the seam allowance on the paper to that on the stitched strip (fig. 11).

Place the ruler over the triangle and cut (fig. 12).

Note the marks on the ruler are so that you can place it down on the other side.

You can also tape the triangle on the back of the ruler to help you.

So, no squares - no problem!

Triangles on a Roll (TOAR)

I used TOAR when making the HST for the quilts. I have given you instructions for making the HST individually and then also for using TOAR (cutting instructions are in blue lettering).

If you asked me what are the three notions that you cannot live without—this is one of them

To help you get familiar with using the TOAR, I will share my process.

Fig. 13

Count how many HST are in each color combination. You may wish to number them as I did in the example (fig. 13). If I am making a lot of different fabric combinations, sometimes, I will count out the triangles and then write the color combination on the paper (it's coming out anyway)

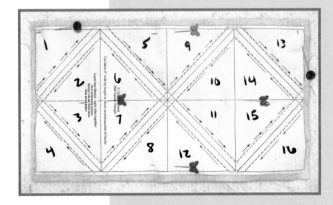

Fig. 14

I prefer to work with a fabric strip slightly larger than the strip of TOAR (that's just my preference—and the yardage calculations for the quilts incorporate this, figure 14).

I also prefer to cut the fabric strip in half and work with a smaller section—feel free to cut and work with the size that you are comfortable with.

After starching my fabrics, I will layer them as follows:

✱ Fabric you are pressing toward (RS up)

✱ Fabric you are pressing away from (RS down)

✱ TOAR paper

Pin away from the dotted lines as you are going to be sewing on them.

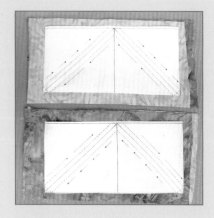

Fig. 15

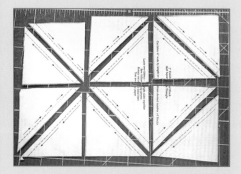

Fig. 16

Fig. 17

Fig. 18

If you will be putting your HST together to form a flying geese unit—such as in Siesta Time or Sands of Time, it helps if you have HST pressed in the opposite directions so that the seams interlock.

To do this easily—make your TOAR sandwich with one of the fabrics against half the amount of triangles required and then make another sandwich that will have the other fabric against the remaining half of the triangle paper (fig. 15).

Cut apart on the solid lines (fig. 16).

Press towards the fabric that is on the bottom with the paper still on. This gives it stability.

Clip the "bunny ears" (fig. 17). Carefully remove the paper (fig. 18). You are good to go!

In a Nutshell...
Working with Triangles on a Roll

1 Purchase "FINISHED" size of the Triangles on a Roll for the size HST you are making
2 Place the fabric that you are pressing towards on the BOTTOM—(RSU)
3 Next place the second fabric (RSD)
4 At this point I spritz with starch and press the two fabrics together
5 Finally add the (TOAR) paper on top and pin down securely.
6 Stitch the HST lickety split
7 Place the stitched fabric onto the ironing surface paper side down and press (you could spritz with starch if you like)
8 Cut the (HST) apart on the drawn lines
9 PRESS the triangles open with the paper still on (for stability)
10 Trim off the little "ears" on the corners and tear off the paper
11 Use 'em!

Connector Squares

The connector technique uses a square, which is placed on a corner of another square or rectangle and then stitched on a diagonal line drawn from corner to corner. The square is then folded back, creating a triangle on the corner. This technique was made famous by the late Mary Ellen Hopkins. It is sometimes referred to as "snowball corners" or "stitch and flip corners".

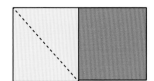

Fig. 19

There are different schools of thought on trimming away the underneath part of the triangle. I prefer to cut away just the middle of the three (3) fabric layers (see figures) so that you can easily line up the adjoining piece and it will not distort the block.

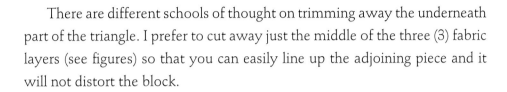

Fig. 20

Using your favorite marking tool, draw a diagonal line from corner to corner on all Connectors.

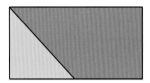

Fig. 21

Place the "connector" square on top of the base square or rectangle (RST). Make sure that the drawn line is going in the right direction. Stitch ON the drawn line (fig. 19).

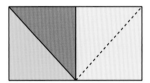

Fig. 22

Cut away the inside of the square approximately ⅛" to ¼" away from the drawn line (fig. 20). Fold the triangle up to match the corners (fig. 21).

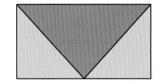

Fig. 23

After pressing the triangle to the corner of the base fabric—repeat on the opposite side (fig. 22)—again making sure that you will be stitching and folding the right direction (fig. 23).

There are several tools on the market today which allow you to create connectors without having to take the time to draw the line. I would suggest that you try a few of them so that you can decide which one works best for you. My particular favorite is the What's My Angle tool. I do not have to draw lines, and I can piece connectors quite fast if I chain them one after another—alternating the direction (fig. 24).

Fig. 24

Fig. 25

Fig. 26

Fig. 27

Strip Piecing

You may think that strip piecing is so easy—just placing two strips together, stitching down the long edge and sub cutting. Some quilters encounter frustrations during the strip piecing process, which I will attempt to alleviate. I have some suggestions that will help you to keep your strips straight!

I will tear the selvedge edges off the sides and then the top and bottom of the fabrics that I am using for strips. This puts them on the straight of grain. Batiks tear the best because of their high thread count.

Starch each fabric lightly and press one on top of the other—lining up the torn edges. Bring both to your cutting mat.

I prefer to work with the WOF cut in half—so approximately 20"–21" pieces. This size is easier to cut, stitch, and press and also is less likely to get "wonky".

Referring to the Power Cutting figures on p. 19—power cut your strips into the designated size.

Stitch with the fabric that you are pressing toward on the top—using a ¼" seam allowance. Do not stretch the strips as you sew, rather let the machine's feed dogs move the strips under the needle.

Spritz with starch and press closed (fig. 25).

Open the strip set on the ironing board with the fabric you are pressing toward next to you. Place the tip of the iron directly to the right of the fabric (fig. 26).

Hold the strip at an angle and gently glide the tip of the iron in the seam allowance along the strip (fig. 27).

Spritz with starch and press the strip open (fig. 28).

If you are sub cutting the strip sets—then take the pressed strip sets to the cutting board and lay them on top of each other (fig. 29).

Power sub cut the strip sets into the designated sizes (figs. 30–31).

Fig. 28

Fig. 29

Fig. 30

Fig. 31

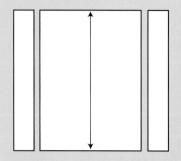

Fig. 32

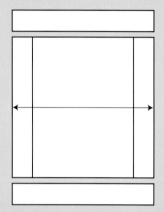

Fig. 33

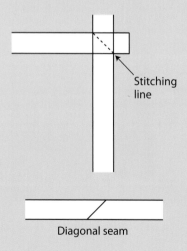

Stitching line

Diagonal seam

Fig. 34

Borders and Binding

Measuring Your Quilts for Borders

Sometimes the size of your quilt can change by the time you reach the final stage of adding borders. This slight change can occur because all of the seams involved in the piecework. For this reason it is a good idea to cut the borders to match your actual quilt and not necessarily the instructions on the pattern you are using.

Measure the center of your quilt lengthwise (fig. 32). Cut your borders to that center length measurement. Attach to the quilt, easing in any fullness necessary.

Measure the center of your quilt widthwise (including the borders you just added (fig. 33). Cut your top and bottom borders to that center width measurement. Attach to the quilt easing in any fullness if necessary.

Tips for Piecing Border or Binding Strips

Try to cut your borders on the straight of grain of the fabric, never on the bias because they can stretch out of shape. If possible, buy enough fabric and cut the borders on the lengthwise grain (parallel to the selvedge edge).

Before you cut your borders, trim off the selvedge edge. The selvedge edge has a tighter weave that you don't want in your project.

When piecing border fabric, sew strips together with diagonal seams (fig. 34). It will be less noticeable then straight seams.

PROJECTS

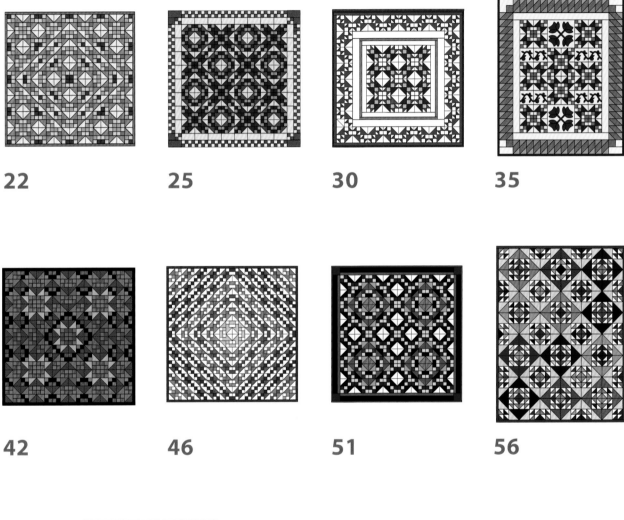

22   25   30   35

42   46   51   56

63   68   74

SUNRISE – SUNSET, 64"x 64"
Designed by Linda J. Hahn
Pieced by Janet Byard
Quilted by Deloa Jones

SUNRISE – SUNSET

Fabric Requirements

1¼ yards cream

1¼ yards red print

⅝ yard coral

⅜ yard green

⅜ yard blue

1¼ yards yellow

⅝ yard for binding *(Your choice of fabrics)*

2¼ yards (2) cuts of each for backing *(This will give you enough fabric for a matching hanging sleeve.)*

Precutting

Fabric	Number of pieces	Size	Method
Cream	64	5" squares	HST
	4	10½" x WOF strips	HST using TOAR
Red	64	5" squares	HST
	4	10½" x WOF strips	HST using TOAR
Coral	8	2½" x WOF strips	Four Patch
Green	4	2½" x WOF strips	Four Patch
Blue	4	2½" x WOF strips	Four Patch
Yellow	16	2½" x WOF strips	Four Patch
Your choice	8	2½" x WOF strips	Binding

Referring to the instructions on p. 12, make (64) HST to yield a total of (128) using the red print and cream

Fig. 1

Referring to the instructions on pp. 18–19, stitch (8) strips of yellow together with (8) strips of coral. Sub-cut the strip sets into a total of (128) 2½" units.

Fig. 2

Referring to the instructions on pp. 18–19, stitch (4) strips of yellow together with (4) strips of blue. Sub-cut the strip sets into a total of (64) 2½" units.

Fig. 3

Referring to the instructions on pp. 18–19, stitch four (4) strips of yellow together with four (4) strips of green. Sub-cut the strip sets into a total of (64) 2½" units.

Fig. 4

Stitch (64) Blue/Yellow units to (64) Coral/Yellow units to make a Four Patch.

Fig. 5. Make 64.

Stitch (64) Green/Yellow units to (64) Coral/Yellow units to make a Four Patch.

Fig. 6. Make 64.

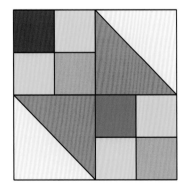

Fig. 7. Make 64.

Referring to the block image (fig. 7), stitch the components that you just made into a total of (64) blocks.

Referring to the image of the quilt (fig. 8), lay out the blocks and stitch together into rows, and then stitch the rows together into the quilt top.

Feel free to rotate the blocks around to come up with your own design for these blocks!

Stitch the blocks together into rows and then stitch the rows together. Layer, baste, quilt as desired, bind and ENJOY! Don't forget the label!

Fig. 8. Quilt Assembly

TIME FOR LOVE – XOXO, 80" x 80"

Designed and quilted by Linda J. Hahn

Pieced by Melissa Winters

TIME FLIES, 68" x 68"

Designed by Linda J. Hahn
Pieced by Anna Marie Ameen
Quilted by Deloa Jones

Time Flies

Fabric Requirements

1 yard purple

⅜ yard blue

¼ yard gold

⅜ yard green

1¼ yards bright red

¼ yard dark red

3 yards cream

⅝ yard for binding
  (Your choice of fabric)

2¼ yards 2 cuts of each
  for backing seamed
  vertically.

Precutting

Fabric	Number of pieces	Size	Method
Purple	16	5" squares	HST
	1	10½" x WOF strips	HST using TOAR
Blue	56	3" squares	HST
	2	6½" x WOF strips	HST using TOAR
Gold	32	2½" squares	HST
Green	5	2½" x WOF strips	Border
Bright red	28	5" squares	HST
	1	10½" x WOF strips	HST using TOAR
	8	2½" x WOF strips	Border
Dark red	16	3" squares	HST
	1	6½" x WOF strips	HST using TOAR
Cream	16	5" squares	HST
	1	10½" x WOF strips	HST using TOAR
	56	3" squares	HST
	1	6½" x WOF strips	HST using TOAR
Scraps	148	2½" squares	HST
	8	3½" x WOF strips	Border
Your choice	8	2½" x WOF strips	Binding

Referring to the instructions on p. 12. Make (16) HST to yield a total of (32) 4" HST of Purple and Cream.

Fig. 1. Make 32.

Referring to the instructions on p. 12. Make (16) HST to yield a total of (32) 2" HST of Dark Red and Cream

Fig. 2. Make 32.

Referring to the instructions on p. 12. Make (28) HST to yield a total of (56) 4" HST of Red and Cream.

Fig. 3. Make 56.

Referring to the instructions on p. 12. Make (56) HST to yield a total of (112) 2" HST of Blue and Cream.

Fig. 4. Make 112.

Referring to the image of the block (fig. 5)—use the 2" Dark Red and the 4" Purple HST along with a 2½" square of Cream and Gold. Make 16.

Fig. 5. Make 16.

Referring to the image (fig. 6)— stitch four (4) of the blocks together. Make (4). Stitch the four (4) large blocks together into the center of the top.

Fig. 6. Make 4.

Referring to the image (fig. 7)— stitch four (4) of the blocks together. Make (4). Stitch the four (4) large blocks together into the center of the top.

Fig. 7. Make 4.

Referring to the image of the block (fig. 8)—use the 2" Blue and the 4" Red HST along with the 2½" squares of Cream. Make (28).

Referring to the image of the pieced border (fig. 9)—stitch these blocks into t w o (2) rows of eight (8) blocks and then two (2) rows of six (6).

Fig. 8. Make 28.

Fig. 9

Add the Borders

First Border: (Cream)

Add 3½" x 32½" strip to each side.

Add 3½" x 38½" strip to the top and bottom.

Second Border: (Green)

Add 2½" x 38½" strip to each side.

Piece three (3) 2½" x WOF strips and cut into two (2) 2½" x 42½" strips.

Add to the top and bottom.

Third Border: (Cream)

Piece three (3) 3½" x WOF strips and cut into two (2) 3½" x 42½" strips.

Add to each side.

Piece three (3) 3½" x WOF strips and cut into two (2) 3½" x 48½" strips.

Add to the top and bottom.

Fourth Border: (Blocks)

Add the six (6)-block borders to the sides.

Add the eight (8)-block borders to the top and bottom.

Fifth Border: (Red)

Piece two (2) 2½" x WOF strips and cut into two (2) 2½" x 64½" strips.

Add to each side.

Piece two (2) 2½" x WOF strips and cut into two (2) 2½" x 68½" strips.

Add to the top and bottom.

Layer, baste, quilt as desired, bind, and enjoy!

Fig. 10. Quilt Assembly

Mornings Glory, 72" x 88"

Designed by Linda J. Hahn

Pieced by Debbie Fetch

Quilted by Deloa Jones

MORNINGS GLORY

Fabric Requirements

⅔ yard dark purple

2½ yards cream

⅔ yard light green

1⅛ yards dusty purple

½ yard gold

1⅞ yards dark green

1 fat quarter red *(flowers)*

¾ yard for binding
  (Your choice of fabric)

2¾ yards 2 cuts of each
  for backing

Precutting

Fabric	Number of pieces	Size	Method
Dark purple	32	5" squares	HST
	2	10½" x WOF strips	HST using TOAR
Cream	32	5" squares	HST
	2	10½" x WOF strips	HST using TOAR
	2	16½" squares	Appliqué
	4	8½" x 16½" rectangles	Appliqué
	6	4½" x WOF strips	Borders
	8	2½" x WOF strips	Four Patch
Light green	8	2½" squares	Four Patch
Dusty purple	68	4½" squares	Border
Gold	68	2½" squares	Border
	4	4½" x 8½" rectangles	Border
Dark green	4	4½" squares	Border
	68	4½" x 8½" rectangles	Border
	Scraps	For stems and leaves	Appliqué
Red	1	Fat quarter for flowers	Appliqué
Your choice	9	2½" x WOF strips	Binding

Referring to the instructions on p. 12, make (32) HST to yield a total of (64) HST using the Purple and Cream.

Fig. 1

Referring to the instructions on pp. 18–19. Stitch the 2½" x WOF strips of Green to the 2½" x WOF strips of Cream.

Sub-cut into a total of (128) 2½" segments.

Fig. 2

Stitch these units into a total of (64) Four Patch units.

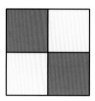

Fig. 3. Make 64.

Referring to the image of the block (fig. 4)—stitch the HST and the Four Patch units into the block. Make (32).

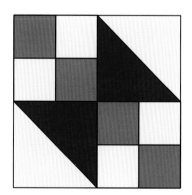

Fig. 4. Make 32.

Referring to the image (fig. 5)—Stitch four (4) blocks together to create a 16" block. Make (8).

Fig. 5. Make 8.

Make four (4) corner blocks by stitching a 2½" gold square to a 2½" green square. Then stitch a 2½" x 4½" rectangle across the top.

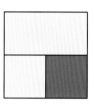

Fig. 6

Referring to the instructions on p. 17—"connector" a 2½" gold square to the left side of a 4½" x 8½" green rectangle. "Connector" a 2½" purple square to the right side of this rectangle.

Fig. 7

Referring to the image (fig. 8), stitch (14) of the rectangles together. Stitch a corner block onto each end. Make two (2) for the top and bottom borders.

Fig. 8

Referring to the image (fig. 9), stitch (20) of the rectangles together. These are the side borders.

Fig. 9

Appliqué

The appliqué pieces in this quilt are suitable for hand or machine appliqué. Since this is not a how to appliqué book, I will only describe the method that we used for this quilt.

The appliqué pieces are fused down onto the background square or rectangle using your favorite fusible web product. There are so many on the market nowadays—you are probably most familiar with Wonder Under, Misty Fuse or Steam-A-Seam. Please follow the instructions on your chosen product for the best results.

Trace the designs (pp. 40–41) onto the wrong side of the fusible web and iron onto the fabric that you will be using for that piece. Cut out the shapes, tear off the paper, and fuse onto the background square.

Stitch around each shape using a straight stitch (raw edge appliqué), zig zag or buttonhole stitch.

You may wish to place a tear away stabilizer underneath your background square to stabilize the block as you appliqué. Remove the stabilizer prior to quilting the top.

To make the wavy stems in the smaller blocks (fig. 11)—fuse a 16½" x 8½" piece of fusible web to a 17" x 9" piece of green fabric. Freehand cut or draw a wavy steam and then cut—choosing how thick or thin that you with the stem to be.

From the scraps of the wavy stem, freehand cut some leaves and fuse them down, again, choosing how big or small you wish your leaves to be.

Once the appliqué is finished on the block and the stabilizer is torn away, you can stitch the appliqué blocks to the pieced blocks and move on to the borders!

Finishing

Referring to the image of the quilt (fig. 12)—stitch the blocks together into rows and the rows into the quilt top.

Piece together three (3) 4½" x WOF strips and cut into two (2) 4½" x 56½" strips. Add these strips to the sides of the quilt

Piece together four (4) 4½" x WOF strips and cut into two (2) 4½" x 64½" strips. Add these strips to the top and bottom of the quilt.

Add a long pieced border strip to each side of the quilt.

Add the pieced border/corner strip to the top and bottom of the quilt.

Layer, baste, quilt as desired, bind , label, and ENJOY!

Fig. 10. Make 2.

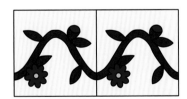

Fig. 11. Make 4.

Fig. 12. Quilt assembly

MORNINGS GLORY
Flower Block A
Make 2
©2016 Linda J. Hahn

Enlarge 250%
This block should
measure 1"

MORNINGS GLORY
Flower Block B
Make 4

©2016 Linda J. Hahn

Enlarge 250%
This block should
measure 1"

MIDNIGHT MADNESS, 64" x 64"
Designed and quilted by Linda J. Hahn
Pieced by Melissa Winters

MIDNIGHT MADNESS

Fabric Requirements

1¼ yards black print

⅝ yard orange

⅝ yard purple

⅓ yard teal

1⅛ yards pink

1⅛ yards green

⅝ yard black

⅓ yard blue

⅝ yard for binding
  (*Your choice of fabric*)

2¼ yards 2 cuts of each
  for backing—seamed
  vertically. (*This will also
  give you enough left over
  for a matching hanging
  sleeve.*)

Precutting

Fabric	Number of pieces	Size	Method
Black print	64	5" squares	HST
	4	10½" x WOF strips	HST using TOAR
Orange	20	5" squares	HST
	1	10½" x WOF strips	HST using TOAR
Purple	36	5" squares	HST
	2	10½" x WOF strips	HST using TOAR
Teal	8	5" squares	HST
	1	2½" x WOF strips	Four Patch
	1	10½" x WOF strips	HST using TOAR**
Pink	14	2½" x WOF strips	Four Patch
Green	14	2½" x WOF strips	Four Patch
Black	8	2½" x WOF strips	Four Patch
Blue	4	2½" x WOF strips	Four Patch
Your choice	8	2½" x WOF strips	Binding

** Cut this strip in half—from the leftover cut a 2½" strip to use for the Four Patch

To make the following HST, please refer to pp. 12–16 and choose your favorite method. You will need the following combinations.

Total of (72) – 4½" HST using Purple/Black Print

Total of (40) – 4½" HST using Orange/Black Print

Total of (16) – 4½" HST Teal/Black Print

Fig. 1. Make 72.

Fig. 2. Make 40.

Fig. 3. Make 16.

Stitch together the following strip sets:

Nine (9) Strips 2½" x WOF – Pink/Green

Sub-Cut these strip sets into a total of (132) 2½" units:

Fig. 4

Four (4) strips 2½" x WOF – Black/Blue

Sub-cut these strip sets into a total of (60) 2½" units

Fig. 5

Four (4) strips 2½" x WOF – Black/Pink

Sub-cut these strips into a total of (60) 2½" units.

Fig. 6

One (1) strip 2½" x WOF – Pink/Teal *(you can cut these strips in half)*

Sub-cut this strip set into four (4) 2½" units

Fig. 7

Now you will stitch the sub-cut units that you have just made into the following Four Patch units

Make a total of (64) Four Patches using the Pink/Green units.

Fig. 8. Make 64.

Make a total of (60) Four patches using one (1) Black/Blue and one (1) Black/Pink

Fig. 9. Make 60.

Make a total of four (4) Four patches using one (1) Pink/Green and one (1) Pink/Teal

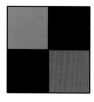

Fig. 10. Make 4.

Using the HST and the Four Patches that you have just made—refer to the image of each block and make the number specified.

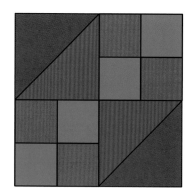

Fig. 11. Make 4.

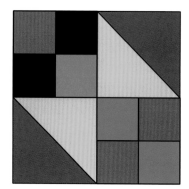

Fig. 12. Make 16.

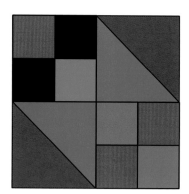

Fig. 13. Make 8.

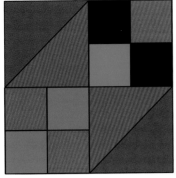

Fig. 14. Make 32.

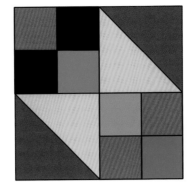

Fig. 15. Make 4.

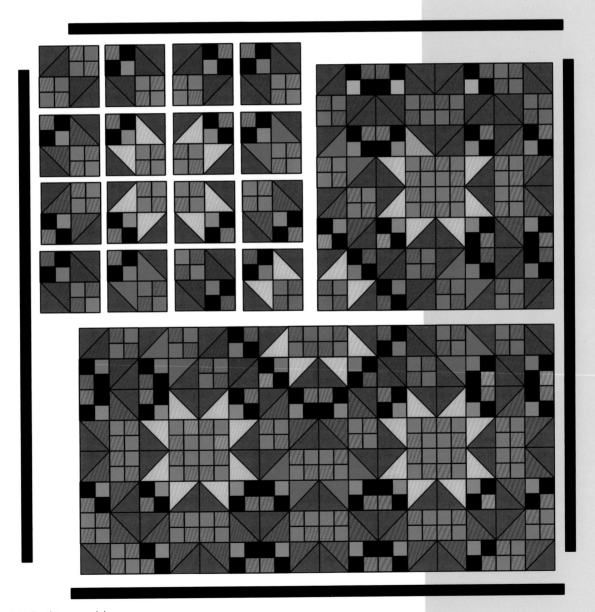

Fig. 16. Quilt assembly

TIME TRAVEL, 60" x 60"

Designed by Linda J. Hahn
Pieced by Debbie Welch
Quilted by Jodi Robinson
Long quarter yard cuts in a rainbow of colors
set in a Trip Around the World layout.

TIME TRAVEL

Fabric Requirements

3 yards cream

¼ yard yellow solid

⅛ yard yellow print

¼ yard orange solid

¼ yard orange print

¼ yard red solid

¼ yard red print

¼ yard pink solid

¼ yard pink print

½ yard pink/purple solid

¼ yard purple solid

¼ yard purple print

¼ yard blue solid

¼ yard blue print

¼ yard green solid

⅛ yard green print

¼ yard teal solid

⅛ yard teal print

⅝ yard for binding
(Your choice of fabric)

2 yards 2 cuts of each
for backing *(Your choice
of fabric)*

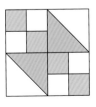

Precutting

Fabric	Number of pieces	Size	Method
Cream	100	4" squares	HST
	5	10½" x WOF strips**	HST using TOAR
	25	2" x WOF strips	Four Patch
Yellow solid	4	4" squares	HST
	1	8½" square	HST using TOAR
Yellow print	1	2" x WOF strip	Four Patch
Orange solid	8	4" squares	HST
	1	8½" x 16" rectangle	HST using TOAR
Orange print	2	2" x WOF strips	Four Patch
Red solid	12	4" squares	HST
	1	8½" x 24" strip	HST using TOAR
Red print	3	2" x WOF strips	Four Patch
Pink solid	16	4" squares	HST
	1	8½" x 32" strip	HST using TOAR
Pink print	4	2" x WOF strips	Four Patch
Pink/purple solid	20	4" squares	HST
	1	8½" x 40" strip	HST using TOAR
	4	2" x WOF strips	Four Patch
Purple solid	16	4" squares	HST
	1	8½" x 32" strip	HST using TOAR

** These strips will be cut into smaller sizes—please refer to the specific size to coordinate with the solid squares.

Precutting (continued on next page)

Precutting (continued)

Fabric	Number of pieces	Size	Method
Purple print	4	2" x WOF strip	Four Patch
Blue solid	12	4" squares	HST
	1	8½" x 16" rectangle	HST using TOAR
Blue print	3	2" x WOF strip	Four Patch
Green solid	8	4" squares	HST
	1	8½" x 16" rectangle	HST using TOAR
Green print	2	2" x WOF strip	Four Patch
Teal solid	4	4" squares	HST
	1	8½" square	HST using TOAR
Teal print	1	2" x WOF strip	Four Patch
Your choice	8	2½" x WOF strip	Binding

The instructions for making the blocks are all the same. Please refer to pp. 12–16 for making the HST using your choice of methods. Refer to pp. 18–19 for making the strips for the Four Patches.

Make 4 Yellow Blocks

You will need a total of eight (8) Yellow Solid/Cream HST.

Stitch together one (1) 2" x WOF of the Yellow Print and one (1) 2" x WOF of the Cream.

Sub-cut into (16) 2" units to make the Four Patches.

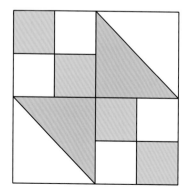

Fig. 1. Make 4.

Make 8 Orange Blocks

You will need a total of (16) Orange Solid/Cream HST.

Stitch together two (2) 2" x WOF of the Yellow Print and two (2) 2" x WOF of the Cream.

Sub-cut into (32) 2" units to make the Four Patches.

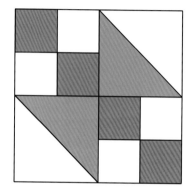

Fig. 2. Make 8.

Make 12 Red Blocks

You will need a total of (24) Red Solid/Cream HST.

Stitch together three (3) 2" x WOF of the Red Print and one (1) 2" x WOF of the Cream.

Sub-cut into (48) 2" units to make the Four Patch.

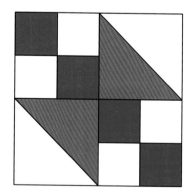

Fig. 3. Make 12.

Make 16 Pink Blocks

You will need a total of (32) Pink Solid/Cream HST.

Stitch together four (4) 2" x WOF of the Pink Print and four (4) 2" x WOF of the Cream.

Sub-cut into (64) 2" units to make (32) Four Patches.

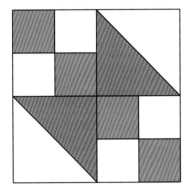

Fig. 4. Make 16.

Make 16 Purple Blocks

You will need a total of (32) Purple Solid/Cream HST.

Stitch together four (4) 2" x WOF of the Purple Print and four (4) 2" x WOF of the Cream.

Sub-cut into (64) 2" units to make (32) Four Patches.

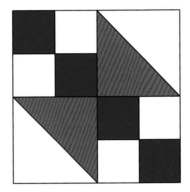

Fig. 6. Make 16.

Make 8 Green blocks

You will need a total of (16) Green Solid/Cream HST.

Stitch together two (2) 2" x WOF of the Green Print and two (2) 2" x WOF of the Cream.

Sub-cut into (32) 2" units to make (16) Four Patches.

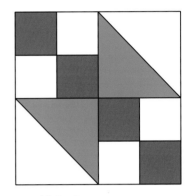

Fig. 8. Make 8.

Make 20 Pink/Purple Blocks

You will need a total of (40) Pink/Purple Solid/Cream HST.

Stitch together five (5) 2" x WOF of the Yellow Print and five (5) 2" x WOF of the Cream.

Sub-cut into (80) 2" units to make (40) Four Patches.

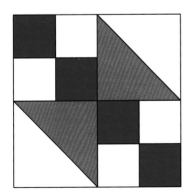

Fig. 5. Make 20.

Make 12 Blue Blocks

You will need a total of (24) Blue Solid/Cream HST.

Stitch together three (3) 2" x WOF of the Blue Print and three (3) 2" x WOF of the Cream.

Sub-cut into (48) 2" units to make (24) Four Patches.

Fig. 7. Make 12.

Make 4 Teal blocks

You will need a total of eight (8) Teal Solid/Cream HST.

Stitch together one (1) 2" x WOF of the Teal Print and one (1) 2" x WOF of the Cream.

Sub-cut into (16) 2" units to make eight (8) Four Patches.

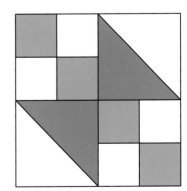

Fig. 9. Make 4.

Lay out the blocks following the image of the quilt (fig.10) so that you get the proper orientation of the blocks. Remember that the Four Patch units form a chain of color around the quilt.

Stitch the blocks together in rows and the rows into the top.

Layer, baste, quilt as desired, bind, and ENJOY!

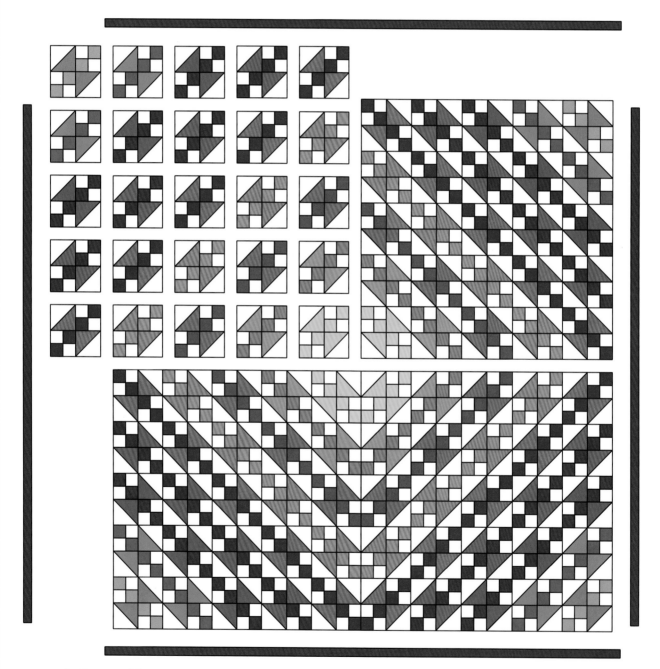

Fig. 10. Quilt assembly

9 TO 5, 72" x 72"

Designed and pieced by Linda J. Hahn

Quilted by Jodi Robinson

FIVE O'CLOCK SOMEWHERE, 64" x 64"

Designed by Linda J. Hahn
Pieced by Deb Stanley
Quilted by Jodi Robinson

FIVE O'CLOCK SOMEWHERE

Note on the Construction of this Quilt

You will be using specific yardage/colors for the center section. For the surrounding block components, you can use the pre-cuts and/or your Stash (since you won't need a lot of any specific color).

I have written the instructions referring to specific fabric colors for the center and then refer to the remaining fabrics as just "colors" so that you can use what you wish to work with.

There are so many colors in this quilt—and you do not need a lot of many of them, we have chosen to make this quilt from yardage and a package of 10" squares. You will be able to strip piece some of the components while others you will need to cut and stitch individually.

Fabric Requirements

3 yards white

⅓ yard orange

1¼ yards magenta

(32) 5" squares colors for center: teal, blue, dark blue, and lime green

(20) 10" squares of a variety of colors*

(2) 10½" squares of teal and lime green

10½" x WOF blue

10½" x WOF dark blue

⅝ yard for binding
   (*Your choice of fabrics*)

2½ yards 2 cuts of each for backing seamed vertically.

Precutting

Fabric	Number of pieces	Size	Method
White	3	2½" x WOF strips	Strip pieced with magenta
	4	2½" x WOF strips	Strip pieced with orange
	32	5" squares	HST *for center with teal, blue, dark blue, and lime green*
	20	10" squares	HST *with variety of colors*
	2	10½" squares	HST using TOAR *with teal and lime green*
	1	10½" x WOF strips	HST using TOAR *with blue*
	1	10½" x WOF strips	HST using TOAR *with dark blue*
Orange	4	2½" x WOF strips	Strip pieced with white
Magenta	3	2½" x WOF strips	Strip pieced with white
Teal, Blue, Dark Blue Lime Green	32	5" squares	HST *with white*
Variety of Colors*	20	10" squares	HST *with white*
Your choice	8	2½" x WOF strips	Binding

*Use the pre-cut package of 10" squares or cut from your stash

Using the 10" squares

You can get two (2) 5" squares which will give you four (4) HST of the same coloring and then eight (8) 2½" squares (fig. 1).

You can get four (4) 5" squares which will give you eight (8) HST of the same coloring (fig. 2).

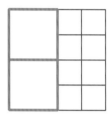 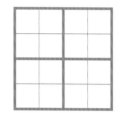

Fig. 1   **Fig. 2**

This quilt is constructed and laid out onto the design wall from the center out.

Please follow the instructions and make all the block components first before placing them onto the design wall.

Making The Four Patch Units

You need a total of (24) Four Patch units of Orange/White (fig. 3).

You need a total of (20) Four Patch units of Magenta/White (fig. 4).

You need a total of (4) Four Patch units of Orange/Magenta/White (fig. 5).

Fig. 3. Make 24.   **Fig. 4.** Make 20.   **Fig. 5.** Make 4.

Referring to the instructions on pp. 18–19 for Strip Piecing.

Stitch a 2½" x WOF strip of Orange to a 2½" x WOF strip of White. Repeat with the remaining three (3) strips of the same color combination. Sub-cut these strip sets into a total of (52) 2½" units.

Repeat using the three (3) 2½" x WOF strips of Magenta and White. Sub-cut these strip sets into a total of (44) 2½" units.

Stitch the 2½" units cut from the strip sets into the required Four Patch units.

Making the Half Square Triangles for the Center

You will need a total of eight (8) HST of White and Lime Green.

You will need a total of eight (8) HST of White and Teal.

You will need a total of (20) HST of White and Bright Blue.

You will need a total of (28) HST of White and Dark Blue.

If you are using 4" Triangles on a Roll (TOAR), those cutting instructions are in BLUE.

If you are using squares, please refer to the instructions for making HST on p. 12 and use the following pieces:

* (32) 5" squares of White
* (4) 5" squares of Lime Green
* (4) 5" squares of Teal
* (10) 5" squares of Bright Blue
* (14) 5" squares of Dark Blue

If using (4" FINISHED) TOAR—please follow the instructions for making HST on pp. 15–16 and use the following pieces:

Fabric	Number of pieces	Size
White	2	10" squares (pair with Lime Green and Teal fabrics)
	1	10" x 25" strip (pair with Bright Blue)
	1	10" x WOF (Pair with Dark Blue)
Lime Green	1	10" square
Teal	1	10" square
Bright Blue	1	10" x 25" strip
Dark Blue	1	10" x WOF

Now that the center block components have been completed, you can begin working on the remaining components.

Please refer to the cutting diagrams in "Using 10" squares" p. 65.

Make the HST components first. You can either use TOAR or you can cut your 10" square into four (4) 5" squares for this portion of the instructions.

Breaking down the remaining block components you will see that the four corner units require eight (8) HST of the same color.

Choose eight (8) 10" squares from your "color" pile and eight (8) White 10" squares. Make eight (8) sets of eight (8) HST.

You will be using four (4) sets of eight (8) HST in the corners and then you will use the remaining HST in sets of four (4) to make up the remaining HST components for the quilt.

From the remaining 10" color squares, choose ten (10) 10" squares and cut each of them into (16) 2½" squares each.

Repeat using ten (10) 10" squares of White.

Stitch one (1) of each of the 2½" color squares to one (1) of the 2½" white squares.

Do not stitch them into Four Patch units until you have the quilt laid out on your design wall.

Start Laying Out the Design

Begin in the middle of the quilt and work outwards. Start by using the Four Patch and HST units that were made from the yardage. Then start adding the HST and the Two Patch units that you just made using the 10" squares.

Referring to the image of the quilt—stitch the blocks together into rows and the rows into the quilt top.

Layer, baste, quilt as desired, bind, label, and ENJOY!

Fig. 6. Quilt assembly

SIESTA TIME, 72" x 72"

Designed by Linda J. Hahn
Pieced by Nancy Rock
Quilted by Jodi Robinson

SIESTA TIME

Fabric Requirements

3¼ yards burgundy
  (includes binding)
1⅔ yards teal
1½ yards copper
1⅝ yards cream
⅞ yard salmon
¼ yard blue
½ yard dusty pink
¼ yard gold
¼ yard apricot
⅝ yard for binding
  (Included in the burgundy fabric requirement)
2⅜ yards 2 cuts of each for backing**—seamed vertically *(This will also give you enough left over for a matching hanging sleeve.)*

**CHECK the width of your backing fabric before you purchase it. Some fabrics have a few inches more than 40" useable width—some do not. If yours does not you will need to purchase another cut of 2⅜ yards or piece a small strip in between the larger cuts to insure that your backing is wide enough.

If you are using TOAR, you will need 2" finished and 4" finished.

Precutting

Fabric	Number of pieces	Size	Method
Burgundy	32	2½" x WOF strips	Borders
	54	3" squares	Small HST
	2	6½" x WOF strips	Small HST using TOAR
	9	2½" x WOF strips	Binding
Teal	36	5" squares	Large HST
	3	10½" x WOF strips	HST using TOAR
	18	3" squares	Small HST
	1	6½" x WOF strip	Small HST using TOAR
	28	3" squares	Border 3
	2	3" squares	Border 3 Corners
	60	2½" squares	Border 5
	8	3" squares	Border 5 Corners
Copper	36	5" squares	Large HST
	3	10½" x WOF strips	HST using TOAR
	28	2½" x 4½" rectangles	Border 5
	28	3" squares	Border 5
	1	6½" x WOF strip	HST using TOAR
Cream	108	3" squares	Small HST
	6	6½" x WOF strip	HST using TOAR
	6	2½" x WOF strips	Border 1

Precutting (continued on next page)

Precutting (continued)

Fabric	Number of pieces	Size	Method
Salmon	18	3" squares	Small HST
	1	6½" x WOF strip	HST using TOAR
	28	2½" x 4½" rectangles	Border 3
	2	3" squares	Border 3 Corner
	28	3" squares	Border 5 HST
	2	6½" x WOF strips	HST using TOAR
Blue	18	3" squares	Small HST
	1	6½" x WOF strip	HST using TOAR
Dusty Pink	36	3" squares	Small HST
	2	6½" x WOF strips	HST using TOAR
Gold	18	3" squares	Small HST
	1	6½" x WOF strip	HST using TOAR
Apricot	18	3" squares	Small HST
	1	6½" x WOF strip	HST using TOAR

Using your chosen method for making HST, pp. 12–16 make the following combinations.

Make (36) Large HST to yield a total of (72) HST using the Teal and Copper fabrics.

Fig. 1. Make 72.

Make (36) Large HST to yield a total of (72) HST using the Blue and Copper fabrics.

Fig. 2. Make 72.

Make (36) Small HST to yield a total of (72) HST using the Cream and Dusty Pink fabrics.

Fig. 3. Make 72.

Make (54) Small HST to yield a total of (108) HST using the Cream and Burgundy fabrics.

Fig. 4. Make 108.

Make (18) Small HST to yield a total of (36) HST using the Cream and Teal fabrics.

Fig. 5. Make 36.

Make (18) Small HST to yield a total of (36) HST using the Apricot and Salmon fabrics

Fig. 6. Make 36.

Referring to the image of the block (fig. 7), assemble the HSTs that you have just made. Make (36) blocks.

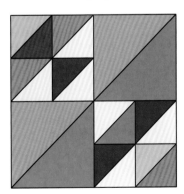

Fig. 7. Make 36.

Assemble the blocks that you have just made into groups of four (4) (fig. 8). Make (9) blocks.

Fig. 8. Make 9.

Stitch these large blocks into rows of three (3) blocks each (fig. 9).

Join the rows to make the quilt top.

Fig. 9

Piecing the Border Blocks

Pieced borders can be stressful at times—trying to keep the pieces aligned. I have found that it is helpful to break down the borders into smaller sections and then join the sections together.

Both borders are constructed the same way just using different fabrics. You will make small sections and then join those sections together.

Once the borders are pieced, you will make and attach the corner HST before stitching the pieced borders to the quilt.

First Pieced Border

Make (28) sections seven (7) for each side of the quilt.

Make (28) Small HST using Teal and Copper fabrics to yield a total of (56) HST.

Referring to the instructions on p. 19 for using Connector Squares—make (28) Flying Geese units using (28) 2½" x 4½" rectangles of Salmon and (56) 2½" squares of Copper.

Referring to the image (fig. 10)—construct a total of (28) sections.

Stitch seven (7) of the sections that you just made together. Make four (4).

Fig. 10. Make 28.

Make two (2) Small HST using the Salmon and Teal fabrics to yield a total of four (4) HST.

Fig. 11. Make 4.

Referring to the image (fig. 12)—stitch one (1) corner square onto each end of two (2) of the border units that you have just made.

These will become your top and bottom pieced First Borders.

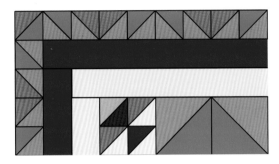

Fig. 12. Corner detail of first border.

Second Pieced Border

Make (28) sections (7) for each side of the quilt.

Make (28) Small HST using Salmon and Copper fabrics to yield a total of (56) HST.

Referring to the instructions on p. 19 for using Connector Squares—make (28) Flying Geese units using (28) 2½" x 4½" rectangles of Copper and (56) 2½" squares of Teal.

Referring to the image (fig. 13)—construct a total of (28) sections.

Stitch seven (7) of the sections that you just made together. Make four (4).

Fig. 13. Make 28.

Make eight (8) Small HST using the Copper and Teal fabrics to yield a total of four (4) HST.

Fig. 14. Make 4.

Referring to the image (fig. 15)—stitch two (2) HST onto each end of two (2) of the border units that you have just made.

Add one (1) 2½" square onto each end of two (2) of these border units.

These will become your top and bottom pieced Second Borders.

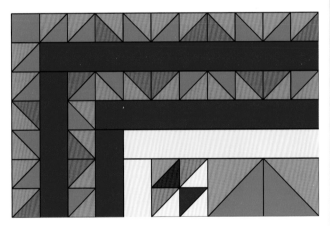

Fig. 15. Corner detail of second border.

Adding the Borders

Piece together seven (7) 2½" x WOF strips of Cream. Cut two (2) 48½" strips and then two (2) 52½" strips. Add a 2½" x 64½" strip of Cream to the sides of the quilt and the 68½" strips to the top and bottom of the quilt.

Piece together eight (8) 2½" x WOF strips of Burgundy. Cut two (2) 52½" strips and then two (2) 56½" strips.

Add a 2½" x 52½" strip to the sides of the quilt and the 56½" strips to the top and bottom of the quilt.

Add the first pieced border units to the quilt. Top will measure 56½" x 60½".

Piece together eight (8) 2½" x WOF strips of Burgundy. Cut two (2) 2½" x 60½" strips and two (2) 2½" x 64½" strips. Add the 2½" x 60½" strips to the sides of the quilt and the 2½" x 64½" strips to the top and bottom.

Add the second pieced border units to the quilt. Top will measure 64½" x 68½"

Piece together nine (9) 2½" x WOF strips of Burgundy. Cut two (2) 2½" x 68½" strips and two (2) 2½" x 72½" strips. Add the 2½" x 68½" to the sides of the quilt. Add the 2½" x 72½" strips to the top and bottom.

Fig. 16. Quilt assembly

RAIN DELAY, 64"x 64"
Designed and quilted by Linda J. Hahn
Pieced by Rebecca Szabo

RAIN DELAY

Fabric Requirements

1⅜ yards light blue

⅜ yard red

⅜ yard brown

¾ yard dark green

¾ yard light green

⅝ yard for binding (*Your choice of fabrics*)

2¼ yards 2 cuts of each for backing. *(You will get a matching hanging sleeve out of this yardage.)*

Precutting

Fabric	Number of pieces	Size	Method
Light Blue	72	4" squares	HST
	3	8½" x WOF strips	HST using TOAR**
	6	2" x WOF strips	Four Patch
Red	6	2" x WOF strips	Four Patch
Brown	6	2" x WOF strips	Four Patch
Dark Green	3	2" x WOF strips	Four Patch
	36	4" squares	HST
	2	8½" x WOF strips	HST using TOAR**
Light Green	3	2" x WOF strips	Four Patch
	36	4" squares	HST
	2	8½" x WOF strips	HST using TOAR**
Your choice	8	2" x WOF strips	Binding

** Cut one strip in half

Referring to the instructions on p. 12, make (36) HST of each color combination (fig. 1).

Fig. 1. Make 36 of each.

Referring to the instructions on pp. 18–19, stitch together strip sets and sub-cut as follows:

Four (4) 2" x WOF strips of Red and Blue.

Sub-cut into (72) – 2" segments.

Fig. 1

Two (2) 2" x WOF strips of Brown and Dark Green.

Sub-cut into (36) – 2" segments.

Fig. 2

Two (2) 2" x WOF strips of Brown and Light Green.

Sub-cut into (36) – 2" segments.

Fig. 3

Before you even think it….. NO, you cannot just reverse these Four Patches. The colors are in different positions.

Make nine (9) Four Patches with the Red/Dark Green on the right (fig. 4) and then nine (9) Four Patches with the Red/Dark Green on the left (fig. 5).

Fig. 4   **Fig. 5**

Make nine (9) Four Patches with the Red/Light Green on the right (fig. 6) and then nine (9) Four Patches with the Red/Light Green on the left (fig. 7).

Fig. 6   **Fig. 7**

Referring to the block image, stitch the components that you just made into a total of (18) blocks nine (9) of each layout (figs. 8 and 9).

Pay attention to the orientation of the Four Patch when doing these!

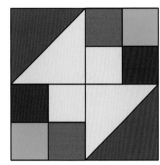

Fig. 8   **Fig. 9**

Now you will be working with the Light Green HST and the Dark Green Four Patches.

Referring to the block image, stitch the components that you just made into a total of (18) blocks nine (9) of each layout (figs. 10 and 11).

Pay attention to the orientation of the Four Patch when doing these!

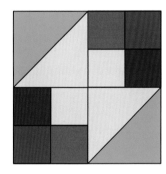

Fig. 10   **Fig. 11**

Lay out and stitch the blocks as follows:

Rows 1, 3, 5—Use the blocks with the Dark Green Large HST (fig. 12).

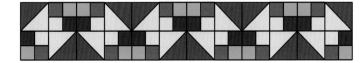

Fig. 12

Rows 2, 4, 6—Use the blocks with the LIGHT green Large HST (fig. 13).

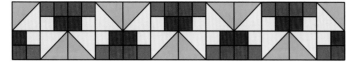

Fig. 13

Stitch the rows together to form the quilt top (fig. 14).

Layer, baste, quilt as desired, bind and enjoy!

Fig. 14. Quilt assembly

Bonus Quilt

SANDS OF TIME, 36" x 48"

Designed by Linda J. Hahn

Pieced by Luanne Halleran

Quilted by Deloa Jones

SANDS OF TIME

always like to try to include a scrap/stash quilt in my books. I have PURPOSELY not included any yardage requirements, but rather I have included the size of the pieces. You can make this quilt in whatever size you choose by simply making more blocks.

You will also be assembling the blocks a little different than the other projects. As the Four Patch units of one block create a secondary pattern. In order to insure that you can easily flow the color placement from one block to another, I have broken down the block assembly differently.

Fabric Selection Note

Throughout this project, I will refer to the lights as Cream (for the large HST) and White (for the small HST) and then the remaining fabrics as Dark.

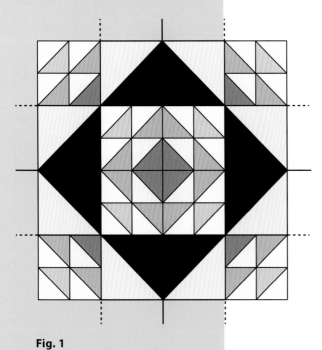

Fig. 1

For my Cream – I used a variety of Cream tone on tones. For my White - I used a variety of White tone on tones.

For the Darks – I used many different colors ranging from Mediums to Darks.

Let's start by breaking down the larger block. This block is comprised of FOUR (4) smaller blocks.

The solid line divides this large block into Four (4) small Hourglass blocks.

The dashed line further divides the Four (4) small blocks into Four components.

When you combine the blocks together, you can see that the smaller components in the corners combine for form the secondary pattern.

So we will now break down and construct the quilt in stages. Laying out and assembling the blocks will be the very last step.

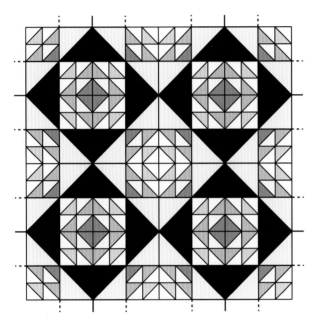

Fig. 2

For this project, I have chosen to use 3" finished and 1½" finished TOAR. If you are not using TOAR, then you will be cutting squares to make your HST. The sizes to cut for TOAR are once again designated in blue.

PLEASE MAKE ALL of the components first— so that you have a nice color selection. If you try to make this block by block, you will make yourself nuts trying to coordinate the color placement.

For this sample, we used *(and you will have some extra if you want to make this larger).*

* 16 Fat Quarters of Dark— variety of colors/fabrics

* 6 Fat quarters of White (tone on tones)

* 6⅛ yards of Cream (tone on tones —make sure you can differentiate creams from whites)

Since you will be working with small pieces of fabric, you have some choices. You may not have a large chunk or fat quarter to work with so I have broken down the components to help you use up what you have. You will make the main block components first—the corner and setting squares are made at the end.

Large Half Square Triangles Per Block

Option 1 (Cutting Squares)		
Fabric	**Number of pieces**	**Size**
Dark	4	4" squares
Cream	4	4" squares
Option 2 (TOAR) Press half the (HST) to the other fabric after removing paper.		
Dark	1	8½" square
Cream	1	8½" square
Option 3 (TOAR) *This is the one I used* Pair Dark & Cream rectangles—one pair place TOAR on top of light, the other pair place the TOAR on top of the dark		
Dark	2	4½" x 8½" rectangles
Cream	2	4½" x 8½" rectangles

Start by Making the Large HST

You will need e i g h t (8) HST for each block. Four (4) of them will be pressed to the darker fabric and f o u r (4) will be pressed to the lighter fabric.

Use 4½" x 8½" pieces of Dark and Cream or you will need f o u r (4) 4" squares of Cream and f o u r (4) 4" squares of a Dark.

Make one (1) combo with the Cream next to the TOAR and one (1) combo with the Dark next to the TOAR for easy pressing (fig. 3).

Please refer to the instructions on pp. 15–17 for making TOAR.

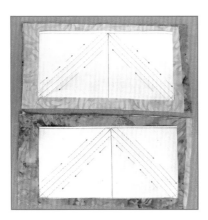

Fig. 3

Stitch together one (1) HST pressed to Cream and one (1) HST pressed to Dark. Press the seam open (figs. 4 and 5). Pin all eight (8) together and set aside.

Make 12 sets f o u r (4) Flying Geese HST units.

Fig. 4

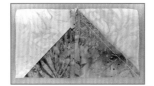

Fig. 5

Small Half Square Triangles Per Block

Option 1 (Cutting Squares)		
Fabric	**Number of pieces**	**Size**
Dark (in groups of 4)	8	2½" squares
White	8	2½" squares
Option 2 (TOAR) Press half the (HST) to the other fabric after removing paper.		
Dark	1	8½" square
White	1	8½" square
Option 3 (TOAR) *This is the one I used* Pair Dark & White rectangles—one pair place TOAR on top of light, the other pair place the TOAR on top of the dark		
Dark	2	3" x 10½" rectangles
White	2	3" x 10½" rectangles

Next Make the Small HST

Pair one (1) 3" x 10½" rectangle of Dark with a 3" x 10½" rectangle of White (fig. 6).

Make two (2).

Make one (1) combo with the Dark next to the TOAR and the other combo with the White next to the TOAR.

Make two (2).

Fig. 6

Use two (2) pressed to the White and four (4) pressed to the Dark and assemble together referring to the image (fig. 7). Press the seams open.

Make (18) Centers and set aside.

Fig. 7

From the remaining (12) small HST:

Pin together two (2) HST pressed to the White and two (2) pressed to the Dark.

Set aside.

From the remaining eight (8) small HST—make four (4) small HST flying geese units.

Pin together one (1) HST pressed to the White and one (1) pressed to the Dark. Stitch together. Press the seam open.

Make (18) sets of four (4)—pin together and set aside.

Here is what my design wall looks like as I am working through the process of making the block components (fig. 8).

This is the 18" mini Cheryl Ann's Design Wall.

Fig. 8

Now let 's build the center blocks.

Select one (1) center, one (1) set of eight (8) stitched triangles and then one (1) set of four (4).

Make 12 blocks (fig. 9).

Fig. 9

These blocks are for the centers of the large blocks. The "setting" and "corner" blocks are made separately.

Make (18) full center blocks (fig. 10).

Fig. 10

Once you have the (18) center blocks made, you can begin laying them out and placing the larger TOAR units around them. You can see in this image how the secondary pattern will form (fig. 11).

Fig. 11

Lay out the entire quilt in this fashion (fig. 12). Once this is completed—you can make the corner and setting squares out of the leftover fabrics.

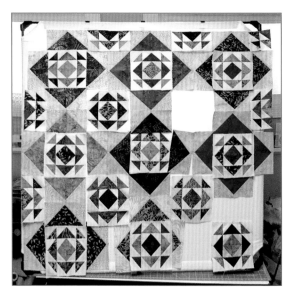

Fig. 12

Now that your quilt is laid out—you will see that there are some empty spaces to fill (fig. 13).

Fig. 13

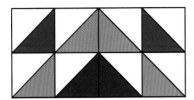

Fig. 14. Make 10 half blocks.

Fig. 15. Make 4 quarter blocks for the corners.

Make ten (10) Half blocks using the leftover HSTs (fig. 14). Make four (4) Corner blocks. Using the leftover small HST (fig. 15).

If cutting using squares, you will need a total of (48) 2½" White squares and (48) 2½" squares of Dark (in groups of two (2).)

Once you have completed making the side and setting blocks you can stitch the quilt top together (fig. 16).

Layer, baste, quilt as desired, and bind! Don't forget a label!

Fig. 16. Quilt assembly

RESOURCES

Piecing Team

Anna Marie Ameen
Princeton Junction, New Jersey

Janet Byard
Lawrenceville, New Jersey

Debbie Fetch
Rushville, Illinois

Luanne Halleran
Palm Bay, Florida

Nancy Rock
Edison, New Jersey

Deb Stanley
Matawan, New Jersey

Rebecca Szabo
Howell, New Jersey

Debbie Welch
Forked River, New Jersey

Melissa Winters
Paducah, Kentucky

Quilting Team

Deloa Jones
South Haven, Michigan

Jodi Robinson
Enon Valley, Pennsylvania

Batting

Nature-Fil™ Bamboo Fiberfill
Fairfield Processing
www.fairfieldworld.com

Thread

50 wt. cotton
Aurifil
www.aurifil.com

Steady Betty Boards

www.steadybetty.com

Triangles on a Roll (TOAR)

www.trianglesonaroll.com

Panasonic® cordless iron

www.americanquilter.com

Cheryl Anns Design Wall

www.cherylannsdesignwall.com

What's My Angle Tool

www.froghollowdesigns.com

Fabrics

Olde City Quilts

339 High Street
Burlington, NJ 08016
www.oldecityquilts.com

Quilting Possibilities

918 Lacey Road
Forked River, NJ 08731
www.quiltingpossibilities.net

BERNINA USA

www.bernina.com

Hoffman California

www.hoffmanfabrics.com

Timeless Treasures

www.fabric.com

Island Batik

www.islandbatik.com

Long Arm Quilters

Jodi Robinson

http://jrdesigns.wordpress.com

Deloa Jones

www.deloasquiltshop.com

Contact Linda to schedule her to come to your guild to Rock That Block!
Linda J. Hahn
www.froghollowdesigns.com; lawnquilt@aol.com
732-792-1187
Facebook—Frog Hollow Designs

ABOUT THE AUTHOR

Linda Hahn is a multiple award-winning author, a sought-after speaker, and teacher at guilds and shows across the country. She began quilting in 1993 and teaching in 1994. Her work has been featured in many of your favorite quilting magazines.

She is a BERNINA Artisan Ambassador, a National Quilting Association Certified Teacher and an iquilt istructor. She was named the NQA 2009 Certified Teacher of the Year. Her first book, *New York Beauty Simplified* (AQS, 2010), was named a bronze medal winner by the 2012 Independent Publisher's Living Now Book Awards and her second book, *New York Beauty Diversified* (AQS, 2013), won the gold medal in 2013. Most recently, her third book, *Rock That Quilt Block: Weathervane* (AQS, 2015), won the gold medal.

Linda's classes are information packed and always full of fun! She clearly enjoys sharing her passion for quilting with her students.

When she's not quilting, she enjoys participating in daily Zumba® classes at her gym. Linda is a licensed Zumba and Zumba Gold instructor.

Linda resides in Manalapan, New Jersey, with her husband, Allan, daughter, Sarah (both of whom are quilters), and her studio helper—a rescue golden retriever named Amber Lynn.

Learn more about Linda on her website, **www.froghollowdesigns.com**, and her Facebook page, **Frog Hollow Designs.**

PHOTO: Glamour Shots, Freehold Raceway Mall, Freehold, New Jersey

Enjoy these and more from AQS

AQS Publishing brings the latest in quilt topics to satisfy the traditional to modern quilter. Interesting techniques, vivid color, and clear directions make these books your one-stop for quilt design and instruction. With its leading Quilt-Fiction series, mystery, relationship, and community all merge as stories are pieced together to keep you spell-bound.

Whether Quilt-Instruction or Quilt-Fiction, pick one up from AQS today.

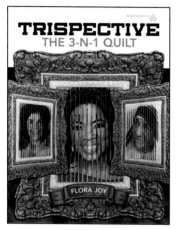

#10281

#10280

#10272

#10283

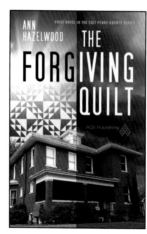

#10279

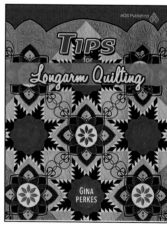

#10285

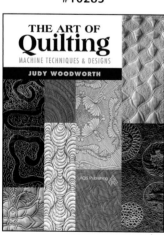

#11140

#10275

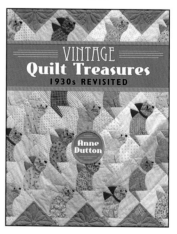

#10277

AQS publications are available nationwide. Call or visit AQS

1-800-626-5420

www.shopAQS.com